Bachelard Interpreted 4

A Flight of Ideas

Frank Prem

Wild Arancini Press
2025

Publication Details

Title: A Flight of Ideas: Bachelard Interpreted Book 4
ISBN: 978-1-925963-24-3 (p-bk)
ISBN: 978-1-925963-72-4 (e-bk)

Published by Wild Arancini Press
Copyright © 2025 Frank Prem
All rights reserved:

No part of this publication may be reproduced, stored in a retrieval system, or transmitted in any form or by any means, electronic, mechanical, photo-copying, recording or otherwise, without prior written permission from the publisher and author.
A catalogue record for this book is available from the National Library of Australia.

Cover Concept: Wild Arancini Press
Cover Image AI assistant: Adobe Firefly

*Who among us has not, on days when he is ambitious,
dreamed of the miracle of a poetic musical prose,
without rhythm or rhyme,
and both subtle enough and abrupt enough
to adapt to the soul's lyrical movements
the undulations of reverie?*

*Charles Baudelaire, cited by Gaston Bachelard
in Air and Dreams*

CONTENTS

A Flight of Ideas

Introduction 1

Air and Dreams

buttercup meadow 5
holding close to beauty 7
storage space 10
hunting a detail 12
full (of sweet words) 14
rid of the truth 15
to dream hospital 19
comparative strength 22
life inside 24
vitae 25
to the ends 28
exploring a new landscape 32
the ladder (part a) climbing 35
the ladder (part b) leaving zero 38
rising blue 41
trip planning 45
the balloon 46
modern times 48
last 50
without a feather 52
wearing down 54
testing (behind the screen) 55
a basket (for his lady) 58
debate at the society for flight 60

the taste of the current	63
hitching	64
no shore	66
backyard latin	68
immigrants	70
the well (1)	71
the stone	74
air china	77
the well (2)	78
the buoy	80
the song of the end (of winter)	82
the well (3)	85
asking	87
a flight of ideas	89
just a thought	92
idee à vivre	95
wings in chorale	96
the weight let go	97
gazing contrails	99
sniffing the scent of a literary flower	101
naturans : naturata	102
there is a 'b' in base	103
o storm	108
an air of punishment	109
mining the sky	111
to fly	114
brother high sister deep	115
street sweep	117
ragpicker	119
out of the attic	121
the climbing wall	124

sky blue question 127
the meteorologist 129
the need of the wind 131
a way away 132
cartography — one time only 133
star balancing 136
scorpion (in the sky) 137
cloud counter 138
rained 141
soup for lunch 142
stone heart 144
the man who loved clouds 146
signs of self 148
future forest 150
daring vertigo — the poplar 151
naked 154
ooo for a voice 156
silently amidst 158
stylish 160
for one 162

Bachelard Source Materials 163

Author Information 165

Other Published Works 167

What Readers Say 169

A Flight of Ideas

Introduction

French scientist and philosopher Gaston Bachelard (1884 - 1962) explored and examined poetics and poetry in great depth over the course of his lifetime, particularly examining the poetics of natural elements, of which he identified the four that are traditionally considered:

Fire
Water
Air
Earth

In addition, however, he (effectively) identified two further elements, or dimensions, for his examination:

Time
Space

The *Bachelard Interpreted* poetry series responds to each of these elements and dimensions, as well as encompassing some of Bachelard's further scientific and literary interests.

A Flight of Ideas takes Bachelard's explorations of the poetic possibilities inherent in dreams and reveries on the lightness of being and weightlessness. It contemplates becoming a balloon, rock climbing among the stars, fantasies of flight. The terrors of disorientation and the absence of any support other than air.

In this collection, the knowledge that one can fly is certain, with the power of dream able to make it so, while also being potent enough to threaten well-being. Possibly requiring a visit to Dream Hospital to aid recuperation.

Note: A *Flight of Ideas* is one of a series of poetry collections inspired by the work of Gaston Bachelard. References to the Bachelard translations that have been relied on as source materials for this project are listed at the end of this book.

Air and Dreams

buttercup meadow

it is an open field

meadow grass
and buttercups

.
.
.

no

a homestead
with an orchard

red fruit hanging
from every tree

.
.
.

no

there —
a road —
a house on this near side
with a wooden fence
shaded white

on the other side
hand-picked flowers
grace matching mounds
and their thin
wooden crosses

.
.
.

no

a car is on the road
flashing past a mall
the local shopping centre

under-ground parking

a trolley lies
abandoned here
on the near side
of this suburban highway

.
.
.

no

no
it is just an open field

only buttercups
in a meadow . . .

.
.
.

he blinks

blinks again

quick-scribbles a note —
written to himself —
then slowly
wanders on

a man at peace
with his imagination
beneath
a warming sun

holding close to beauty

if I dream you
just right
you will have magnificent wings
with which to fly

but . . .

how can I
let myself
release you

.
.
.

scissors

or shears

I must stretch
your so-beautiful
white wings

it is your *remiges*
I must cut
those snow feathers
that I dreamed

to keep you close
my darling one

~

you are no longer
in any way
useful

you are not
beautiful
any more
poor crippled thing

there is no place now
for *you*
in my imaginings

once
I thought you
the height
of all my grace

my elegance
and poise

I
said you

spoke your name
in my mind
beneath my breath

you fired my soul
you were my light

but now you are
just . . .

here

you do not soar
you do not fly

I look
but cannot see
you
as once you were

I know I know
I know
it was me
who cut your wings

I know
that it was me
who tied you to the ground
but
what of that

A Flight of Ideas

I did what I must do
and now
I will
again

what choice
have I

it is my nature

storage space

she contemplates

> no
>
> no room
> in the bedroom . . .

crates and boxes
everywhere she looks

underneath the beds
is taken

it is the same in the hall

the linen closet
is filled with containers

odd shapes and sizes
strange ties
and means of containment
everywhere

it is no good
she will have to consult
an architect

perhaps
she should extend the house
upstairs

build an attic
or a basement

either way

something
must be done

A Flight of Ideas

there is no space
no room
to be creative
and it needs to be addressed

this house
has no remaining capacity
to store her ideas

she must have
another room

hunting a detail

I am chasing a nuance
over
to the dark side

around the curve

the hunt
leads
to shadings
but *I*
illuminate
each step
upon the way

and what was dark
is enlightened

what was hidden
is clear
except . . .

my nuance has
now
scurried further
into shadow

I adjust the helm-light
and am
again
hurrying in my pursuit

again
just behind the quarry

if I can catch it . . .

I will see
nuance
in the day

A Flight of Ideas

no subtle
differentiations

no *degrees* . . .

much less
overtones

away away
the hunt is on
for the nuance
and the subtle refinements
of all its kind

full (of sweet words)

he wrote a line

bent low down —
sniffed —
until he could taste it

    high

wrote another line —
another stanza —
read the words aloud

declaimed them

    high

he crazed
across a lined page —
such cheap
cheap paper —
his words so dear . . .

smelt them

said them

drank them *in* and drank them *up*

he is now so overfull
of sweet words
he is a drunkard

a hophead
a user
a pusher

he
is so
high

rid of the truth

everything he said
became true

realization came
only gradually
and
it is apparent in hindsight
that —
when he was younger —
he sometimes made
mistakes

but with maturity
came clarity

a certainty of voice —
of expression —
that he could not suppress
and —
over time —
he realised

at first
he set tests for himself

made outrageous declarations

> *concocted*
> *random utterances*
>
> *spoke*
> *streams of consciousness*

all true

his questions
became
philosophical proofs

his idle speculations
the basis for further
fruitful
investigation

he became noticed

> *sensationalised*

> *nationalised*

and began watching
behind himself
and peeking
around corners

he said
he had become
paranoid

that he felt
people were observing him
all the time

> *testing him*

> *plotting*
> *his exploitation*

> *discussing him on television*

it was true

only in his thoughts —
unuttered —
did he feel safe

he isolated for a day
locked and alone
in a room

without once speaking

A Flight of Ideas

felt almost faint
with relief
that he had not spoken
a true word
all that day

then spent another day
identifying the corners
of a plan

he announced

> *I will hold*
> *a news conference*
> *for the press of the world*
> *to attend*
>
> *to hear me speak*

when all were gathered
he announced

> *I will tell you now*
> *three things*
> *that are true*
>
> *I am going away*
>
> *you will not know*
> *where I have gone*
>
> *you will not follow me*
>
> *I am able*
> *to speak lies*

he left the podium
and walked
alone
from the building

returned
anonymously
to his home

and was not troubled
again

that
is the truth

to dream hospital

somebody wake her family

    beep

tell them
she's sleeping

    beep

~

these people
are professionals

they know the signs
to watch for

oneiric-para-medicals
have done all this
before

~

put in a line

insert the canula

    beep   *beep*

let's feed her
by naso-gastric

    beep

strap her down —
firm —
onto the gurney

beep   *beep*

you never know . . .

she might just have
a wild one

beep

or she could be stuck
inside
for days

beep

~

they won't wake
her

not here

they'll take her
to the slumber ward

~

beep

look
can you see her eyes
move

something's happening
in there

beep-beep   *beep*

beep-beep   *beep*

now
we just have to wait

A Flight of Ideas

beep

did somebody wake
the family

do it now
tell them . . .

tell them
that she's fast asleep

and all systems
are normal

stabilised

beep

beep

beep

~

these people
are professionals

they have done
all this
before

comparative strength

I am strong
I am
of the earth

I hear the slow melodies
of the underworld
as it moves

I reach deep

at least as deep
as I stand
tall

the earth and I —
we —
will not be moved

~

> *you are strong*
> *I know*
>
> *I have touched*
> *your boughs*
>
> *no-one can make you move*
>
> *I know*
>
> *rest awhile*
>
> *I will rustle your leaves*
> *with my song*
>
> *rest*
>
> *rest*
>
> *as I sing you*
> *and*
> *we sway*

A Flight of Ideas

sway and bend

move with me
while I sing aloud

the song that turns
to storm

back and forward

can you lean
any further

blow blow

blow

I will blow
and you

will fall

life inside

the sign on the door
read

> *office vacant*

the note
on the desk stated

> *occupant*
> *away*

the sticker —
self-adhering
to her forehead —
read

> *I'll be back*
> *in five*

but over the top
of that note
another had been pasted
to state

> *that isn't true*
>
> *she's gone*

gone a long time

imagining
dreaming
living a life
inside

vitae

through the morning
his agitation
grew

he had done what he could
to distract himself

emptied the six-sided
old bottle —
left to sit
so long forgotten
on the shelf —
with its few
brief
and unrelated phrases
remnant within

he had swallowed those
in a single mouthful

nothing

he had then
pulped —
liquefied to a purée —
an old novel

decanted the black
from the grey

shaken it . . .

swallowed

.
.
.

still nothing

no more than a dross
of undistinguished
and unmemorable ink
that had never been used
to pen beauty

or
to tattoo a flower
onto a page
in her true colours

a mere
almanac

a *word salad*
with no
dressing

.
.
.

he needed
a fresh bottle

    new-distilled

    cleansed

    black

    gleaming

    only ever used
    on poetry

he needed to ingest
his
substance vitae

A Flight of Ideas

by mouth

intravenous

misted in a gas

he didn't care
but
for the love of god
he needed to take in
a good poem

~

when they found him
he appeared normal
enough

no jitters
or twitches

rational

lucid
in conversation

it was only . . .

only his eyes —
the irises —
that looked odd

it was remembered
they had been the colour
of sky —
blue

but now
they were pale
as the shade
of a thin
grey
cloud

to the ends

there be monsters

.

.

.

here be monsters

the map showed the detail —
the *where*
at which he was standing —
while he studied

this
his beginning point
~

when he focused
on the X
that marked himself
he saw

his house
his street
his home

all that he knew

the dotted path
began
right there

a line drawn
away from his feet
to lead
with an arrow

to show him the way

A Flight of Ideas

to
another place

    . . . be monsters

    .

    .

    .

    there
    be monsters

he followed the path
followed the line
and followed the arrow
that pointed
ahead

everywhere he passed
he gazed about
at wonders

at the new

saw
what looked *familiar*
dressed
in gaudy colours

and moved on

pursued
the dotted line

everywhere
everywhere
was a place never seen . . .

was a place
just the same as . . .

everywhere

the map
showed words
at his feet

said

> *here*
> *is where you are*

and he *was*

halfway from the start

half
to the end

> *there be monsters*

the map had never
showed
a lie

> *here be monsters*

but how would he *know*
when the journey
had ended

> *there be monsters*

nothing so very unusual
but
everything seemed brand new

> *here be monsters*

was it stranger
where he'd *been* . . .

A Flight of Ideas

or stranger
where he was
going

    . . . be monsters

exploring a new landscape

there are safety rules

*you will have to
wear your helmet
at all times*

*there might be
patches of darkness*

even tunnels

*you should test
your halo-lights*

now
please

*also however
you may
at times
need to have your goggles
handy*

*some of the bright spots
will seem intense*

*you must respond
to what you see
and what you feel you need
but –
in any case –
be ready*

*this is a fresh terrain
and nobody
has been as close
as you and I will be
on this expedition*

A Flight of Ideas

*we will be attached
by a rope
strung between my waist
and yours*

*firmly secured
to each of us*

*if you go down
I go down*

remember that

*it will be my job –
and only mine –
to insert the pitons
on the occasions
when we need to climb*

*we will be crossing
areas of rock
of ice
and of snow*

*any of these areas
can be sharp
and slippery*

unpredictable

*there may be sections
that rise and twist
sharply*

*or break off
completely*

your boots are the best

*they have good grip
but you must take care
where
you place your feet*

this landscape
has not been seen
before
so we can't guarantee
your safety
in all areas

there may be
unpleasant
surprises
as well as vistas
of splendour
of every hue

stick with me
stick with the rules
and we'll be
be fine

now
are you ready

let's do this

let's explore some art

the ladder (part a) climbing

there is no light

there is no
gravity

there is only
up

and no way to know
in which direction
that might be

~

he holds to a steel rung
of the ladder

climbing
the darkness

maybe
climbing higher

pauses —
one arm looped
around a stanchion —
takes some nourishment
a little relief

laughs

a small
brittle
sound

    so
    which way
    does north lie . . .

it was important
once
but now he might be east
or
going west

god help him
even south
again

he thinks

>   *well*
>   *you have to*
>   *have a chuckle*
>   *don't you*

though
it sounds more like
the rasp of a breath
fed through
a one-way valve

and he has to
hold on
lest he float

a

w

a

y

~

he clutches a rung

pretends he knows where
north
is illuminated
on the map that he holds
in his head

A Flight of Ideas

and starts to climb
again

the sounds
of his boots
on the metal
ring hollow

the ladder (part b) leaving zero

he has . . .

what
exactly

not fallen . . .

drifted . . .

descended . . .

tumbled —
out of control
in slow motion —
from
some mighty distance
above
to . . .

eventually . . .

sort of clatter
sort of crash

kind of
bounce

until
he is now
no longer moving

A Flight of Ideas

he had reached
the heights
by climbing

clambering
on rungs
incessantly

forever

and now —
even in the darkness —
he knows
his ladder is there
at a right-angle
to where he lies

and his ladder
is also *there*
on the opposite
angle

just as ready
to be climbed

the surface
he has alighted on —
and grips so tightly
to stop any possibility
of further fall
or drift —
is the ladder

waiting

and beyond
the upright that forms
the right-angle
leading back
to where he has been . . .

yet another ladder
lying flat
waits
to be climbed

he cannot see them
in the black
but
he knows
and
his decision
is a reduced one

forward or back
up or down

positive
or
negative

he searches —
a little desperately —
within himself
rummaging the various axes
in his mind
to intuit
the best way
to leave zero

rising blue

it began
as a slow-moving patch —
no bigger
than a carpet square —
of colour

blue

walking through
a solid darkness
it was a bright
glimmer
that caught his eye

he
and the colour
approaching each other

it moved like liquid
and looked like paint
but
as it curled
up
and around

over
his feet

it behaved more
like smoke

when he bent
to run his hand low
through the substance
there was
nothing

only colour
and air

as he walked further
the hue rose
seeming to sever his legs

his knees

he could move
freely
but the landmarks

> *road*
> *curb*
> *shrubs*
> *handrails*

one by one
disappeared

the colour climbed
halfway
up tree trunks

as high
as his shoulders

he could hear
the rushing water
of the creek
that ran below a bridge
just a little way
ahead of him
but
he could not
go forward

unimpeded
yet
he was frozen
in place

A Flight of Ideas

encompassed
by the rising sea
of blue
that he could not touch

could not
penetrate

he found himself
holding his breath
as the colour —
which he could not smell
or taste —
reached his mouth . . .

covered it

and climbed higher
over his nose
his eyes

when he inhaled
at last
it was through an explosion
of coughing
that retched
emptily

he waved his hands
but could not disturb
the airy solidity
of blue

stumbling forward
with arms
outstretched
he found —
fell into —
the protective guardrail
of the bridge

slid to the ground
to sit

with his back secure
against the structure

he stilled his ragged
breathing
to listen . . .

nothing

only the sound
of running water
below him

at last —
his eyes irritated
and dry from a prolonged
unblinking
stare —

he allowed his eyelids
to close

and found
his vision

all the lost surroundings

still there
in front of
his tightly closed
eyes

clear and sharp
within their sweet
natural
darkness

without awareness
of doing so
he began to weep

trip planning

    we could hike
    or we could drive

    we could fly

    let's go and hire
    some wings

    I'll fit yours on tight
    then I'll turn around
    and you
    can fit mine
    to me

    one-two-three
    we'll start to flap

    one-two-three
    we will run . . .

    take off
    into the open air

    would you like that
    would you like
    to travel
    like that

    we could fly

the balloon

he placed the end
to his lips
and exhaled

    his dreams

exhaled

    his hopes

exhaled

    his longings

with the breath
of himself
he inflated his balloon
until
it was tight

ready
to be released

to seek a home
up
in the clouds

and he placed . . .

    his faith

with the last —
the very last —
breath
he held

A Flight of Ideas

knotted the end
and . . .

released

knowing —
with certainty —
it would float
high up
and away

so light
it would never
let him down

so light
that
all it could do
was raise him

higher

modern times

sceptic
and cynic

she sets a monument —
an altar
of sorts —

inside it
she places her soul

turns
to all the quarters
and summons
the demons

>   ali dahka

>   beel-zebub

>   div-e sepid

>   freud

but they
don't do
much

root around with fire
or
jab ineffectually
with lances
thoughts
and foul intentions

they don't come
close

she turns to mythology
and summons

A Flight of Ideas

magi

djinn

shamans

and witches

    jung

offensive cackling

putrid exhalations

hopeful incantations

they dance
and build
magic fires

psycho-analysed
exhaustively

but none . . .

none
can find the strength
the potency or power
to move
her poet soul

last

what is
a last breath

she imagines a scene

>*ice-light*
>
>*blackness and blue-white*
>
>*a grizzled figure —*
>*male —*
>*lying on his back*
>*with hands folded*
>*over his chest*

she can almost feel
the imposing dead-weight
of the folded hands
and arms
across her own chest

restricting the freedom
of diaphragm and lungs
to take in
the necessary quota of air

and as she watches
in increasing self-discomfort

>*a white mist*
>*rises*
>*from the pale mouth*
>
>*suspended*
>
>*for a moment*
>
>*thins . . .*
>
>*disperses slowly*

A Flight of Ideas

is that
it . . .

maybe

but she wonders too
if it isn't also the gradual
stifling
and suffocation
of choices made

narrowing with age
and the barely-suppressed
awareness
of an unswayable
forward creep
towards infirmity

the tease
of fleeting memories
whose laughter
she hears
each day
and feels more
and more
pointedly

more distantly

what is it
really

    the last breath

she doesn't know
not really
but . . .

she can imagine

without a feather

look
I know

all right?

I know

but what else
could explain it?

I've looked —
you
know I have —
and I can't find any trace

as far as I can reach
it is only
skin

I can feel my shoulders
and —
even when it's obvious
that's all there is to find —
I try again

I look in the mirror
with my back to it

I contort
but there *aren't* any

no down
no bristle
no barb

nothing

A Flight of Ideas

but
it happened
I know
that it happened

it was *so* real

and I
flew

wearing down

through the morning
she watched
the creation of a cloud

from traces
glimpsed on the horizon . . .

slowly
sailing forward . . .

growing

billow
upon billow
of feather-filled
soft curves

high on high

an accumulation
of roundness

voluptuating beauty
in low sun

a seduction
wearing
down

testing (behind the screen)

that
is a *scratch*-ing sound

he claws his fingers
drags them down
a line
on the barrier screen

compares
what he *hears*
with what he *heard*

.
.
.

a softened *clomp*

surely that
was a pounce
on carpet

he pounces —
too flat-footed —
pounces again
more accurately

.
.
.

that though
was a shuffle

shush shush
he pushes his feet
backward and forward
sharply
across the carpet

before he has finished
a hollow
tap-ping
perhaps a knuckle
on an empty desk
or a cupboard

.

.

.

a *smash*

some sort of crockery
broken

he has no cup
to compare with
and in any case
that

boing

has to have been
some sort of spring . . .

it's too fast
it's all too fast
and he can't *see*
what the sounds
really *are*

can't know
if what he is doing
is anything like . . .

oh
that was surely
the **[slap]**
of a flat ruler

it is too fast
he can't . . .

A Flight of Ideas

he sinks to the floor

his back
to the screen

hands
covering his ears

how can he know
anything
if he cannot test
what he hears

cannot
see

a basket (for his lady)

in the early pre-dawn
he attached a cuff
to both his hands
and
to his feet

bade her
take her place
inside the basket

and when he had moved —
a small distance
away —
commenced
deep breathing

~

ballooning
at a personal level
is not always
the most comfortable

the expansion is havoc
on clothing
and
stretched and tightened skin —
the contorted head
and gross misshape
of the body —

well . . .

but that
and the endurance
of the slow recovery
back
to his usual form
is a price

A Flight of Ideas

and he knows he will pay
willingly
for the chance
to take his lady

~

another breath

another breath

he is quite suitably inflated
now
barely holding
to the ground

so

he stamps a foot —
stamps it hard —
and pushes
to lift
off the ground
into the gentle breeze

a little higher . . .

and then the basket
with his lady
too

and away
they sail
towards the colours
of the rising sun

debate at the society for flight

the discussion raged

she had listened
first to one side

the merits —
the obvious and patent
merits —
of the feathered path

> adhere them
>
> change diet
> to grow them
>
> flap them
>
> submerge the pilot
> into the middle
> of a container of them
>
> clutch them in hand
>
> clutch them
> in heart
>
> design them anew
>
> enlarge them

proponents had come
and gone

some —
perhaps sadly —
not to return

A Flight of Ideas

and she had listened
to the more complex
other side
of the debate

> *the evident need
> to shed weight
> and to alter substance*

> *to become aesthetically
> slender*

> *remain exteriorly unchanged
> but to lighten —
> somehow —
> the spirit*

> *eat only the flesh
> of sky creatures
> and thus to —
> again some-how —
> change the density
> of land-based bone*

> *alter the patterns
> of thought*

> *the possibilities
> of buoyancy aloft*

she held no beliefs
or convictions in support
of either group

but
it amused her immensely
to listen

even to provoke
the strands
and the vehemence
of their arguments

for she *knew*
the secret

the way

and at night
in her solitary cot
when she closed her eyes

she soared

A Flight of Ideas

the taste of the current

how fast
is the flow
of the wind
I am creating

I may poke
my tongue inyo the air
to re-measure the tang
of my speed

>*turbulence*
>
>*luff and fluff*
>
>*surge*

nothing can stop me
flying

my body
stretched
horizon-wise

flat-out
and dynamic

>*fast air*
>*o*
>*kiss me kiss me*
>*a current*
>*all over*
>
>*you storm*
>*of my own making*
>
>*I*
>*taste you*

hitching

he has a sturdy suitcase
and wears a backpack —
bulging —
with supplies for the road

has waited patiently
for awhile
but there has been
no sign

no indication

and now
he is leaning back —
eyes closed —
against his luggage
in a deep reverie

.

.

.

when the first faint stirrings
ruffle his shirtsleeves
it takes him
a moment
to focus

then he straightens up
grasps the suitcase handle
tight
with one hand

thrusts
the other arm
out to the side

makes a sort of open fist —
thumb at half-cock
and a finger held straight out —
against the breeze

A Flight of Ideas

as the zephyr
turns into wind
and the wind
begins to howl
along the desolation
he can feel it curl
around him . . .

as though
in mid
making-up-it's-mind

a gust at his back
causes a folding of legs
at the knees

he is seated

and at last
they are away

he has hitched a ride
to wherever
the wind
might take him

a ride to
wherever else
that current
might go

no shore

the sky
has no shore

it is an ocean

I
am a swimmer

from cloud —
I swim —
to cloud

I can breaststroke

or
freestyle

I might lie
upon my back

>*breeze currents
>take me*

>*I want a journey*

>*across
>the sea that has
>no shore*

it is
the sky
I
the bird

from cloud
I . . .

.
.
.

A Flight of Ideas

to cloud

the speck
so far sojourning

to
no shore

backyard latin

the dragonflies

the sky

the sun behind

a dancefloor —
suggested —
in the air

tango sharp
they are

they are   here

then

there

how did they learn
to dance in air
like this

slow
slow
and quick-quick

then a slow

> *my dear*
>
> *let me . . .*
>
> *around you*
>
> *I-will-stay-close*

A Flight of Ideas

a dragonfly tango

the dragonfly tango

> *I float*
> *above you*
> *then*

> *it's down*
> *I go*

a dragonfly tango
the dragonfly tango

I fly beside you
then

I go

immigrants

tonight
the stars have drifted off
and wandered
like so many
tiny migrant boats

afloat
on a wide black sea

listen to their song
of

      go – o – going

they sing of *going*
endlessly

the night
is a sky-sea
filled with travellers

they are going
so far

going
endlessly

the well (1)

she is a-twist
at the end of a rope
in the black
no-where
of the well

the dark below
is so solid
she could persuade herself —
almost —
that she might land
there

find purchase
for her feet

but as she watches them —
dangled
in a slow twirl —
she knows
that the only *solid*
is the colour
and
it will shape-shift
to leave a space
she can never
traverse

above
the black is pricked
by a pinpoint

the rope is a solid thing
where it rises
before her eyes

but it dwindles —
so fast —
into the suggestion
of a thin
flaxen thread
that might be an illusion
of non-sense

a *noir* mirage

she touches her nose
to the tautness
of the rope
seeking a reassurance
that *it* —
at least —
is real

her breath sounds loud
in her ears
as she breathes it

a moist echo of itself
within the aura
of her hopelessness

she long ago shouted
until the sound —
reverberating —
grew hoarse
and became no more
than a *croak*

    . . . *roke*

  cro . . .

she wonders
if the well
is the

    what is

A Flight of Ideas

when you die

has she died . . .

what is *death*
down here
alone

regardless
she feels
the deed
is already done

the stone

for fun
he would throw stones

sometimes skimming —
jumping halfway —
across the lake

frighten a duck

sometimes
at a bottle
on a stump

see if he could add
a shard or two
of brown
to the jags
of lemonade
and blue
and green

mostly
he threw long

down the road
to
out-of-sight

or
all the way
across the lake

watching for a water flop
or a puff
of lucky dust

the other side

A Flight of Ideas

yes
he could throw
a bit
for fun

and sometimes
a smooth rounded piece
of white quartz
up from the river
would perfectly fit his hand —
his finger-hold —
just so

special stone

and he would set his eyes
on the blue

limber his arms
so as not
to put
his shoulder out

and then throw

straight up

straight at
the sky

up
above the trees

up
through the clouds

up
into the blue

into the black

~

for fun
he would lie outside
on good nights

picnic rug
on the ground

lie back
and quarter the sky

waiting

  ssshhheeeeeeuuuuuwwww

  ssshhheeeeeeuuuuuwwww

waiting
for his stone
to come back

for a little bit
of fun

  ssshhheeeeeeuuuuuwwww

A Flight of Ideas

air china

> *I ain't a-gonna break*
> *at least*
> *until I hit the floor*
>
> *ain't a-gonna break*
> *at least . . .*

it was a little like . . .

no
it was *exactly*
like flying

what matter
if it came from
a slip
a push
a fall

a leap

the rushing of the air
was an
exhilaration

and the song
a spontaneous joy

short lived but
oh
such life
such fast fast
life

> *I ain't a-gonna break*
> *at least*
> *until I hit . . .*

the well (2)

it is a constant
almost permanent
brightness

a gleam

especially as it shines —
solitaire —
in this deep shaft
of absence

a wet ripple
mirroring the light
of nothing
but
a white glisten

she has twisted . . .

turned . . .

spun

but there is no source
she can locate

all else
is ebon darkness

solid

the light looks
like thin
water
crossing slowly
from the *up*
to the *down*

A Flight of Ideas

progressing endlessly
without seeming
to move
yet shining a mobile
reflection

there was a time —
it seems an age
ago —
when *it*
was *not*
but
she has become
accustomed
now

and its sudden absence

unanticipated
unannounced

unreplaced

is like a physical blow

she strains to see
to hear

there is nothing
but her own sodden
gulp
of air and sound
and
a slow extension
of the trail
of a tear

the buoy

I swim

among the stars
so many
eyes

I take care
to not collide
with these stellar
buoys

I swim

the void
supports me
like a bubble
of uncertainty

which way which *where*
should I go

I swim

the tide
of night-jet
washes me
at last
up
onto the gentle slope
of morning

good day

*good day
mister sun*

A Flight of Ideas

my swim —
with the coming
of the morning light —
is over now

so many have been
the eyes
that have watched
over me

me
the bobbling buoy
among the stars

Frank Prem

the song of the end (of winter)

come

to me

I am your singer

I am your song

it has been
a long winter

come
raise your eyes

sing
with me

yes
it has been a long winter

rain . . .

rain
and

there has been snow

sing
sing with me

such a weighty burden
of weariness

fell on you

with each coating

of new frost

A Flight of Ideas

>   *come along*
>   *now*
>
>   *lift your head*

~

all I want
is to sleep
is to slumber on
through the grey

right through
the short light
that is winter

now
this bird

>   *sing*
>
>   *raise yourself*
>   *into the new light*
>   *and sing*

this chirping bird
sings of light
and of sun
that is come again

a resurrection
of
spirit

>   *sing*
>
>   *I will sing*
>
>   *sing along*
>
>   *sing along*
>   *with you*

perhaps
that was the last
of old winter

the bird

      sing . . .

      sing . . .

the bird
perhaps
is more aware . . .

maybe it knows
more than me

much more
than me

      sing along

goodbye
old winter

the well (3)

she had wept

she had
spoken aloud

screamed
into the darkness
once
or twice

and when —
finally —
she had exhausted herself
fell silent

became still

even her breath . . .

just
a whisper

.
.
.

a feeling

reverberation
like
a tremor

up through her body
to her ears —
her *hearing* —
where it echoed

the sense of a sound
risen
from nowhere

that came
and went

a throb
seeping out
from the walls
of darkness

and a call
that was the vibration —
the *voice* —
below

filled her
with a touch
that was a riffling
of her shirt

into her chest

she closed her eyes
to *feel*

asking

he stood

atop the headland
a sheer slope
down
to the distant sea

raised his wings

raised
his head

    I wish

he spoke —
his voice
contained —

within

    I wish
    with you
    to ride

    I would leave
    this earth
    behind me

    leave it
    below

    wind
    oh
    wind

he ran
some few paces
along the edge
of the land

wind

*hear me
oh wind*

*will you allow
that I should ride*

a tousling
of pinions

a cool breath
from the wide

he turned
to face again
the sky
and the waters

one step —

the air

the ride

a flight of ideas

he caught them
one at a time

one each day
mostly

sometimes more
but . . .

sometimes . . .

none at all

he thought them
beautiful
and examined each
with care
trying to take in —
to absorb —
the essence of them
into his conscious mind

carefully
he placed them
all together
adding one at a time
as he caught them

he half-hoped
that some kind of
kismet
might cause one or more
to combine

to create something greater

eventually
though
it was enough

he felt
they were becoming
crowded

becoming —
perhaps —
a little crazy

~

his favourite place
at the end of winter
was a hilltop
overlooking a valley
filled with early morning fog
and mist

spread
like a quilted blanket

a grey bedspread

it was there
he took them

opening the container
he gently tilted
and placed it
onto its side

first one

then more

finally
all

A Flight of Ideas

like a flocking
of colour
and wonder
rose
into the air

as he watched
they drifted
further

away

until he realized —
after a while —
he was alone

it was time
to go home

just a thought

it came on the back
of a large truck

held down
on all sides
by ratchet straps

reversed into
an unloading bay

released
then lifted ungently
into the air
by a forklift truck

scooted
across the warehouse
to a corner
where it unobtrusively adjusted
itself
to form sides
that matched the right-angle
of the wall

and waited

.
.
.

he approached
clipboard
paper
and pen in hand

stood and looked at it

sniffed . .

testing

A Flight of Ideas

made a note

touched it
detailed the way it yielded
a little
when pressed

from the belt at his waist
he produced a tape measure
for
he had determined
that the proportions
of the thing
seemed deceptive

the dimensions —
sometimes —
appeared to have changed

finally
he approached
until he was almost touching it
with his face —
adjusting eyes and distance
so that he could still see
without blurring —
and he concentrated
on just looking at it

intensely

.
.
.

time
must have passed

must have . . .

he shook himself
to regain focus
and gazed around him

eventually
he noticed the space —
an emptiness —
where it had been

where now stood
only a slatted
wooden pallet

yet he . . .

somehow
he felt
that *he*
was filled to the brim

almost overflowing
and . . .

he had
something . . .

there was *some thing*
that he badly needed
to do

idee à vivre

the idea
had a life
of sorts

beyond just
writing
on a page

beyond
words conjured —
while pondering —
and then
released

it had
a little existence

a spark —
perhaps —
of being

a little thought
a little life
a little
motion

movement
with a small impact
on a little world

for a moment
a *being*

it was . . .

a little idea
à vivre

wings in chorale

this time
the wings are singing

filling all the air
with a hum
that is a bee

that sounds
like a wasp

that is ladybird

dragonfly

a grey heron
rising up from the ground

the madness the whirr
of two red-eyed pigeons

the wings are singing
vibrations

timpani the day
in the key —
the very shrill key —
of cicada

wing song
on a summer day

the air sighs
and is itself fulfilled

A Flight of Ideas

the weight let go

he fell
because he must

there was a point
when the weight
of himself

> *what he had done*
>
> *who he had been*
>
> *all that he had felt*
>
> *the things*
> *he concealed*
>
> *every love he'd had*
>
> *every hate*

added up
to more ounce
and
more pound
than a man . . .

than *this* man
could stand

he fell
all the way
from the top

fell
through the middle

fell completely until
down

he attempted
to work a slide-rule
to calculate
how far
was the fall

but
before he could conclude . . .

start
became *end*

and the weight
felt to be
beyond
his measure

he hugged himself
close

held himself
tight

and let it go
at that

gazing contrails

he circled
a circle

contrail
in the sky

wherever he flew
below him was the earth

effortless
in air
aloft
on the wind

in the vortex

and everything
below
was the ground

someday
oh someday
perchance the wind
may lower him . . .

perchance
perchance
down
to the earth

but now —
for now —
he circled

circled the circle
contrail
the sky
and around

~

she walks
with her head
up
in the air

always
her gaze
on the blue

upon the clouds

the lazy
love you

formed in contrails
in the sky

the easy
luff
around and round

maybe one day
if she learns well
how to leap

maybe one day
the earth
will fall behind . . .

that
is *maybe*

and that is *one day*

but now
she is on the ground
and walks

head pointed
to the sky

A Flight of Ideas

sniffing the scent of a literary flower

I read
in a book
about a flower
with a perfume
as strong
as summer

and though I searched
through pages
by the score

and sniffed

at all the tomes
in all the libraries

and their
shelves

the yellowed stacks
of first editions

I sniffed
yes
but never smelled
the flower
that I once read
described

the scent
of summer

naturans : naturata

it is
what it must be
and is itself
enough

it does
what it must do
because
it is
what it is

would you have it
be something
else

what
would it become
then

would it do a thing —
some
any thing —
that it didn't need
to do
because of what
it had become . . .

no
it would do
what it must do

all
that it must do

because
it *is*
and that
must be
enough

there is a 'b' in base

it began
of course
when he was still outside
looking —
a long look —
up
to the very top
of the building

disconcerting enough
was the movement
of clouds
against such a distant
stationary object
so many storeys high

gradually
as his awareness narrowed
and focused
he understood
that the building itself
was moving —

swaying

giddily —

back and forward
in a strong wind
hinted at
but not felt
from where he stood
on the ground

before the sensation
had settled
he was inside the building

its elevator

he paused
a thoughtful moment
then pressed
the highest button
with the largest number
printed on it

the sense of movement
was almost immediate

a wobble
and then
a feeling of heaviness
pressing
slightly
down on him

and the knowledge —
the sure knowledge —
that he was in a small box
hurtling
towards the sky

the slow
the stop
was a moment
of
himself
catching up
to himself
in fractions

and another wobble
to finally halt
the ascent

seconds
of disorientation
as he stepped
from his small mobile room
onto the exposure
of the roof

A Flight of Ideas

here

the wind
announced itself

> *a whistle*
> *around his ears*
>
> *a grab*
> *tugging at his clothing*
>
> *and the palpable tremor*
> *conveyed viscerally*
> *through the roof*
>
> *rocking*
>
> *here*

the clouds
became a scuttling neighbour

he blocked it
out

all of it

all the sensations shouting at him
of vulnerability

blocked all
except the inner discomfort
of a nauseous unsteadiness
while standing
perfectly still

a few minutes only
to check gear
to lift and adjust the pack
comfortably
onto his back

then careful steps

one

.

.

.

two

.

.

.

three

to the edge

~

the horizon is beautiful
in the distance

closer there are fields

roads

suburbs

taller buildings

below him —
immediately below —
there is a silent voice
a call
speaking into his gut

telling him

>   *jump*

>   *come to me*

>   *fall*

a twisting vertigo
almost dizzying him
to a stumble

A Flight of Ideas

almost
dragging him down

eyes up
eyes up

focus
on the distance

deep breaths

ready

ready

ready

he leaned forward
and
leaned forward

responded now
to the voice in his gut

I come . . .

and leapt

arms
legs

    suit flaps

    opened wide

rippled
and flew
across the city

across *his* city

o storm

o tempest

o storm

rage
your defiance

I cower
undefended

bent
beneath your lash

master destruction

your songs
on the wind
are all cold

I am frozen

dirty water
is you

swirling darkness
is you

shrill the night

uproot the day

flay my soul
till I quake
and I quiver

o tempest

o storm

A Flight of Ideas

an air of punishment

the judge addressed her
from behind
the bench

>*your trial
>is now concluded*
>
>*it has been shown
>without a doubt
>that you are guilty
>as accused*
>
>*it falls now
>to this court
>to pronounce sentence . . .*
>
>*with regard to
>Element
>we have determined:*
>
>*Air*
>
>*with regard to the nature
>of that Air
>it shall be:*
>
>*Heavy*
>
>*you are sentenced
>to go forth
>carrying with you
>a personal surrounding
>of your punishment*
>
>*worn as close as a fitted suit
>of clothing*

*this surrounding
of Air
will be weighted
as heavily –
as densely –
as each of your misdeeds
warrants*

*go forth now
as well
as you are able*

become a better person

slammed the gavel
once

the sentence
was applied

~

free to leave
yet
weighted down
by the past

the hardest act
of her new life
was to stand up
unaided

to take the first
step

mining the sky

she walked —
a weary trudge —
towards the beginning
of her rostered shift
below

every day
the same

dirty toil

danger

darkness
but for the light
of the lantern
perched on her helmet

she hardly noticed

the habit of work
down in the depths
was ingrained

automatic

it required no engagement
of her brain
to wield a pick
and extract the stones —
the dirt —
in the cramp
that comprised her workspace

even as she began
the descent
in her mind
the *focus* was
on rising

she pictured herself
soaring

circling up
on a thermal

massive wings
wide spread

pictured
the blue of the sky

the white-yellow orb
of the sun

felt the wind

flying

she saw *herself*
as though
on the ground
looking up

and
she saw *herself*
as a tiny movement
on the ground

in her mind
she was a creature
of air

held the vision
as she crawled
to her rockface

and only heeled her focus
to the present
when the lantern
raised a gleam
from the wall
before her

A Flight of Ideas

and the sound of the pick
was not the dull thud
of smithed metal into raw earth
nor the sharp
too-loud
ring of the point
striking a rock

but a clear
soft

    clink

that was the solid call
of reward

to fly

she applied herself
to the rehearsal routines

learning to crawl

    practice

learning
to walk

    practice

learning to run
to leap

    practice

learning to climb

    practice

to dance

    practice

    practice and
    practice

to know
how to fly

brother high sister deep

he climbed high

    she sank deep

he wanted the above

    she craved below

mountain ranges rising up

    mountain ranges dropping down

he wanted to go

    she wanted to go

high

    deep

it is hard to see
inside a cloud

    it is hard to see
    where there is no sun

it is hard to breathe
when there is no air

    it is hard to breathe at all
    when the pressure is so great

the brother wore
only white

*the sister wore
darkest black*

the colour high

the colour deep

brother up

*sister
down below*

street sweep

today his arms
move slowly

his feet can do
nothing more
than shuffle

    shuffle

his eyes are nowhere
near his broom

I believe he is dreaming
while he sweeps
time
away

dreaming
from one push —
one swish from
side-to-side —
to another

he is dreaming
and his arms
move slowly

dreaming
as he makes a hill

    a mountain

    perhaps
    touching clouds

    maybe
    there is snow

out of dust
and street debris

I think he is dreaming
to the intersection

>   *the goat path*

>   *the crossing*

>   *the ford*
>   *across the river*

at the end
of the street

ragpicker

ragpicker
ragpicker

what's that
on your back

> *it is a sack
> filled with worries
> and woes*

ragpicker
ragpicker

why
are you bent

> *my bag is heavy
> with burdens*
>
> *I bow low*

ragpicker
ragpicker

are those
the wrong things
that you've done

> *they are only
> what I
> can carry*
>
> *the bigger sins —
> the greatest crimes —
> wear me*
>
> *flesh on their bone*

ragpicker
ragpicker

how much
can you bear

> *I*
> *can bear*
> *nothing*
>
> *but*
> *am allowed*
> *no*
> *respite*

ragpicker
ragp . . .

> *enough!*
>
> *enough*
> *of your chatter*
>
> *my sins are my own*
> *and I carry them*
> *as well as I can*

A Flight of Ideas

out of the attic

> *rummage*
>
> *jettison*
>
> *assess the weight*
>
> *rummage*
>
> *jettison . . .*

she is in her attic
where the old emotions
were once
carefully —
safely —
stored away

out of sight
and unable to exert
any influence

> *in and out*
> *of beribboned boxes*
>
> *strips of no-longer-adhesive*
> *tape*
>
> *item by item*
>
> *emotion*
> *by emotion*

she rummages them out . . .

the confusion
of a child
disciplined

> *jettison*

the disappointment
of a first refusal

    jettison

it is a
painful
process

trying to decide what
if anything
should be kept . . .

a prize
for a school essay

    retain

the clever idea
that changed her workplace

her workmates

    retain

it is painful
but
her soul has grown
heavy

she has felt
dragged down
by the weight of things
she can no longer see

no longer feel

has become
slow

un-spontaneous

A Flight of Ideas

now
with each item
jettisoned
she feels lighter

with each emotion
retained she is a little more
buoyant

and feels
somehow
as though . . .

as though there is
more *room*
inside herself

perhaps

perhaps
she will once again
have the space —
the emotional space —
to breathe

the climbing wall

she had been
in training

now
she was ready

> *helmet*
> *sticky-sole shoes*
> *half-gloves*
>
> *water*
>
> *belay rope*

her finger
found the first
moulded support

held her body weight
while her feet
found —
solid —
their first contact point

and so
inched
from support to support

hitching
and releasing
knots

higher

the vertical ascent
was demanding
physically
and mentally

A Flight of Ideas

and her concentration
intense

    focus
    narrow

    hand support
    to hand support

    foot
    to foot

    up
    and up

she had only vague
awareness
of the ebbing of light

the emerging dominance
of darkness

    hand
    to hand

gradually
changes to the nature
and structure
of the wall —
to the supports —
became apparent

    foot
    to foot

but only when she
raised
her concentration

broadened focus

only then
did she realize . . .

> *the handholds*

> *the footholds*

she was climbing
stars

sky blue question

the question
puzzled him

how

he wondered

how could he capture
the blue
of the sky

from where he stood
on the firm ground
the colour
seemed to be
everywhere
beginning just above
his head

but
reaching up
he could grasp . . .

nothing

he altered vantage

from the modest height
of a nearby hill
the blue . . .

the blue remained
where it had been

just outside the scope
of his reach

rising
in the basket
of a balloon
he could reach out —
precariously —
and clutch . . .

nothing

an airplane showed him
blue
all around
but
no way to reach it

a rocket ship
left the blue
behind

below

the question puzzled him

how could he capture
a piece of the sky

a piece
of the sky-thing
called *blue*

the meteorologist

it is painstaking work

> *how much blue*
>
> *white*
>
> *black*
>
> *how much*
> *purple*
>
> *perhaps gold leaf*
> *or silver*
> *around the edges*
> *as a lining*

it is watercolour work
of course

> *a light wash*
> *of grey*
>
> *shadings*
> *using the blue*
> *and the black*
>
> *voluptuous curves*
>
> *watery streaks*
>
> *shapes*
> *painted atop*
> *shapes*

and she knows
very well
that they won't
stay still
for her

so she must brush
fast
and keep up with them

for
the *front*
wants to move along
to keep just ahead
of the colourless
wind

but
they are shapes
voluptuous enough —
now —
to hold water

if there must
be rain
well
these clouds
will do the job

and so
she puts away
the paints
the brushes
the smock and raincoat

it is time
to study the charts
again

to work out
when
and where
she will next need
to paint
the weather

the need of the wind

it is a need
of the wind
to create beauty

> *breath*
> *on a bud*
> *to haste a flower*

> *ruffling of feathers*
> *to urge a bird*
> *to sing*

> *blowing the bell*
> *to make*

> *ding*

> *dong*

> *dan*

to make a melody
it can carry
away

singing

a way away

I drew a line
to join together
four stars

I named them
constellation

and every night now
I see
my line
through the darkness

I trip from star
to star

tightrope
the cosmos

and then
sometimes
I draw again

another line

I step
further along

my constellation
enlarged
while *I* . . .

am a little more
distant

and farther away
from home

cartography — one time only

it was an act
of dedication

each night
when the moon allowed

when the clouds
allowed

he took his geometry tools

> *a book for drawing*
> *ruler*
> *protractor*
> *pencils and pens*
> *a desk*
>
> *the telescope*

meticulously
he plotted
and charted
star
after star

focusing first
on one —
measuring the distances
and angles —
to the next one

detailing as he went
the size

the colour
of each
compared to its neighbours

he noticed
that —
sometimes —
he could detect patterns

shapes that formed
among the brightnesses
and positions
of different stars

gave them names

night after night
he plotted

charted

until finally
he felt he had finished

had mapped
the universe —
as seen from his desk —
completely

with his own
personal tools

he sat back
and looked up
at the unbroken
blackness
of the night

no sparkle
no twinkle

an empty
darkness

he was surprised
but then
remembered

A Flight of Ideas

his charts
and his maps
had recorded it all

and was
satisfied

star balancing

draw a line
from *sirius*
to *betelgeuse*
to *procyon*

a highway
from point to point
across the night

with
tightrope
and pole
draw *me* there
now

star-balanced
against a black sky

scorpion (in the sky)

antares
beat red
my heart

take fire to *shaula*
take bite and sting
to *lesath*

antares
beat red
and red my heart

dschubba
shine from my forehead
triple light

show the way
shine the way
across heaven

jabbah nu
graffias
ainiyat
sargas
will of the cosmos

god

the mystery

I am you
are me
scorpion sky

I
am you
are me . . .

we
are the scorpion
in the sky

cloud counter

    205

    206

    20 . . .

shhh

do not disturb him

~

he is standing
with a pad
and a pen in hand

craning his head
upwards

counting aloud
and placing a corresponding mark
on his pad

it is a day
of winds and breezes
blowing different strengths
different rates

at different levels
between the ground
and the sky

the vivid blue
of the heavens
is broken
and the sun
periodically obscured
by the passage
of a constant migration
of clouds

A Flight of Ideas

crossing the heavens
from south
to north

from south-west
to north-east

in blobs and billows

in feathers
and curlicues
swirled around
like wispy apostrophes

230

231

23 . . .

he is counting them

recording the clouds

trying hard
not to miss any

to determine
whether a broad spread
of cotton fluff counts
as *one*
or
as *many*

on this day
with a procession occurring
unceasingly
above him
he has his work
cut out
to keep up

accuracy
is important
when clouds
have to be counted

249

250

25 . . .

shh

don't disturb him

rained

she started
by gathering mists

pummelled and shaped
a small cloud

watched it float
away

but the second time . . .

> *perhaps too much?*
>
> *perhaps
> too heavy?*
>
> *too black?*
>
> *too wet . . .?*

it hovered

hung in the air
above her

rained

soup for lunch

it was clear weather
in the dining room
above breakfast

the sun shone

> *eggs on toast*
> *yolks unbroken*
>
> *golden yellow*
> *on white*

a cheerful meal

but the day
deteriorated
became grey

at lunch
a cloud hovered
over the table

seeming to wait
until everyone had gathered —
ready to start —
with the tureen
still covered
in its place
on the table

then
it began to rain

> *pooling water*
> *in the bowls of each spoon*
>
> *making a raised*
> *topography*
> *on the blades*
> *of the knives*

A Flight of Ideas

soaking the bread

*saturating
the table cloth . . .*

papa suggested
they wait it out

mama tried to push it
off to one side
but her hands
went straight through . . .

came out
wringing

the cloud and its storm
remained

mama said

    that's IT!

she leaned into —
through —
the downpour
to seize the tureen

    come on

    *grab your plates
and bring your utensils*

    *today
lunch will be taken*

    in the kitchen

stone heart

I
am the stone
set at the heart
of the crossways
of the universe

I lift my voice
for the wind
to take

>*whispered*
>*loud*

>*whistled and moaned*
>*to the stars*

so that they know

WASH OVER ME
OR WALK BY

CHANGE –
WHEN YOU MEET ME –
THE WAY
YOU WOULD GO

I AM THE STONE

turn slow
turn around
every-north
looks south
and away

from the heart . . .

it is
from me
you
must go

A Flight of Ideas

take my voice
to the stars
as a shout

as a call

take the memory
of me
as a stone

set
at the crossways
of the heart
of
the universe

the man who loved clouds

well

he said

who wouldn't love them

*they are
a transport*

a delight

he considered for a moment
then

*take
the flying carpet*

*do you
for a moment think
that
is really
a floating bit
of stitchery*

*no no
I don't think so*

he wore a small smile now

marvelling
at the ignorant

and the home of the gods

*where do you think
you might find
the home
of the gods*

A Flight of Ideas

    why

    it's up there
    in the clouds

    isn't it

he laughed aloud

    ah
    but —

    seriously —

    aren't they
    just a marvel

    you can never see the same one
    twice

    always changing

    evolving

    big billows

    angel wings

    streaks
    and pointillist dots

he gazed up
at the clear blue
of the sky

    I wish
    I could see one
    again

signs of self

she gazed
at the oak

still and straight

still
and angled

alive . . .

imperceptibly

only showing
gradual changes
from year
to year

> *leaves budding*
>
> *in full green*
>
> *brown*
> *and fallen*
>
> *a girth*
> *wider*
> *than a year ago*
>
> *small branches*
> *decayed and dead*
>
> *small branches*
> *new grown*
> *and alive*

she watched the oak
seeing no sign
of awareness

A Flight of Ideas

but knowing
the slow movement
of sap and water
taking place
inside

hidden

> *the wind*
> *at play with leaves*
> *in the canopy*
>
> *flexibility*
> *in the face*
> *of the irresistible*

she looked at the oak
and saw
herself
as though in a mirror

shook her head
turned back
to the work
in the garden

future forest

from a litter
of gumnuts

ripened on the tree
then released
to the ground

she gathered one

shook from it
a peppering
of seeds

gazing
at the scatter
across her palm
she could —
almost —

see

almost smell

a future forest
of blue-gum

daring vertigo — the poplar

he knew
he was being
foolish

the risk . . .

enormous

but
the attraction

the thrill . . .

undeniable

he approached
the majesty
of the trunk
carefully

keeping his eyes
focused
on the girth

such a girth

positioned himself —
in vertical parallel —
as close
as he could manage

> *took a deep breath*
>
> *took another*
>
> *hugged himself*
> *for luck*

then
tilted his head
bringing his eyes
in line
with the rise
of the trunk

straight up
and diminishing
in a disappearing line

> *end of tree*
> *beginning*
> *of sky*

above . . .

the dizziness
of racing clouds
that made the trunk
seem to revolve
in circles
inflicting an acute sense
of vertigo

nausea

it was beautiful

it was
too much

he was unable
to keep
his footing
anchored

with a cry —
a diminishing
fading
cry —
he fell

A Flight of Ideas

into the sky

lost
among the grey wool
of a passing cloud

naked

she shut down
shut out
the sound

quieted movement

>*the radio*

>*the shop assistant*
>*rattling goods*
>*behind the counter*

>*the customer*
>*requesting*

>*the bread machine*
>*slicing*

>*the cappuccino maker*
>*grumbling*
>*in the corner*

>*traffic*
>*driving past the door*
>*on the road outside*

>*a distant rumble*
>*of thunder*
>*descending from above*
>*through a thick black blanket*
>*of cloud*

then silenced
too
the rain

.
.
.

A Flight of Ideas

listened
to discern what was left
to hear

> *the sound of air*

> *the sound*
> *that was her breathing*

the *in* of it

the *out*

the sound that was
her heartbeat

> *lub dup*

they call it

> *lub dup*

again

and from this place
in the centre
of her own silence
she felt the world
wash away

until
she was left
naked

until she released
a soft sigh

ooo for a voice

he gave up
the potential
of his voice

in a sacrifice
to the wind

reconciled
to his personal silence

~

the wind blew

    oooo-ooo-ooo

the wind blew

    oooo-ooo-ooo

in a voice
that sounded
with his own timbre

that he could *sense*
resounding deep inside

and he felt
that he could whisper
as the breeze did

felt *himself*
within the storm

that he could roar

    ROAR!

~

A Flight of Ideas

speaking as the wind
he gave up
the potential
of his voice

silently amidst

seated

quite still
in the silence
of the work room

manuscript paper
open
blank
on the desk

eyes
open . . .

but
unseeing

he was
still

quite

still

a finger movement —
like a trembled tic —
was the first sign

followed by a sensation —
slowly insinuated —
of tension
that spread
through the room

a tautness

his eyes
now —
could be seen
to be moving

A Flight of Ideas

darting

and the fingers
of his hand
began to twitch
rhythmically

in a sudden movement
he reached for a pen
and began to notate

hardly more
than dotted squiggles

>   *quavers*
>   *semis*
>   *breves*
>   *ties and slurs*
>
>   *beams and dots*
>
>   *caesuras*

he held still
in his mind
each instrument
while he committed
chosen companions
to the paper

the room was silent
apart from the frenetic
scratching
of pen across paper

but he
was in the midst
of symphony

stylish

she imagined herself

a large thing

vague

lumpen

poked
at a point
on herself

>*smoothed it*

>*removed an edge*

>*shaped it*
>*and bevelled*

imagined
herself
more sleek now

more sculpted

imagined
perfection and
she
its embodiment

patted the image —
patted
herself —

was pleased
with what she imagined
now

A Flight of Ideas

then stepped
outside

all class

all style

for one

she drew a mouth

drew
an ear

wrote a dialogue
for the one
to tell
to the other

a story

and
she drew an eye
for one
to see the world
unfolding

Bachelard Source Materials

Gaston Bachelard, French Philosopher lived from 27 June 1884 to 16 October 1962. The series of poems and poetry in this book has drawn inspiration from the following publications by Bachelard, translated into English.

Intuition of the Instant by Gaston Bachelard (1932) Eileen Rizo-Patron (Translator) Northwestern University Press, 2013

The New Scientific Spirit, by Gaston Bachelard (1934), A. Goldhammer (Translator) Beacon Pr; 1st Edition (1984)

The Psychoanalysis of Fire, by Gaston Bachelard (1938), A.C. Ross (Translator) (1964).

Lautréamont, Gaston Bachelard (1939), Robert S. Dupree (Author), James Hillman (Author), Dallas Institute Publications; Reprint Edition (2012)

Water and Dreams: An Essay on the Imagination of Matter by Gaston Bachelard (1942), Edith R. Farrell (Translator) (1983.

Air and Dreams: An Essay on the Imagination of Movement, by Gaston Bachelard (1943), Edith R. Farrell (Translator), Frederick Farrell (Translator) Dallas Institute Publication Dallas Institute Publications (1988)

Earth and Reveries of Will: An Essay on the Imagination of Matter by Gaston Bachelard (1943), Kenneth Haltman (Translator) Dallas Institute Publications (2002)

Earth and Reveries of Repose: An Essay on Images of Interiority by Gaston Bachelard (1948), Mary McAllester Jones (Translation), Dallas Institute Publications (2011)

Dialectic of Duration. Gaston Bachelard (1950), Mary McAllester Jones (Translator), Rowman & Littlefield Publishers; (2016)

The Poetics of Space by Gaston Bachelard (1958), Maria Jolas (Translator) Penguin Classics (1964).

The Poetics of Reverie, by Gaston Bachelard (1960), Daniel Russell (Translator) Beacon Press; New Ed Edition (1971)

The Flame of a Candle, by Gaston Bachelard, (1961), Joni Caldwell (Translator) Dallas Institute Publications (1988).

The Right to Dream by Gaston Bachelard (1970), J.A. Underwood

(Translator) Dallas Institute Publications (1988)
Fragments of a Poetics of Fire, by Gaston Bachelard, Kenneth Haltman (Translator), Dallas Institute Publications (1988)
On Poetic Imagination and Reverie, by Gaston Bachelard, Colette Gaudin (Translator) Spring Publications; (2014)

Author Information

Frank Prem has been a storytelling poet since his teenage years. He has been a psychiatric nurse through all of his professional career, which now exceeds forty years.

He has been published in magazines, online zines, and anthologies in Australia, and in a number of other countries, and has both performed and recorded his work as spoken word.

He lives with his wife in the beautiful township of Beechworth in North East Victoria, Australia.

Connect with Frank

Find Frank at his website www.FrankPrem.com, or through Social Media online at Facebook, X (Twitter), Instagram and YouTube.

Other Published Works

Free Verse Poetry

Small Town Kid (2018)
Devil In The Wind (2019)
The New Asylum (2019)
Herja, Devastation - With Cage Dunn (2019)
Walk Away Silver Heart (2020)
A Kiss for the Worthy (2020)
Rescue and Redemption (2020)
Pebbles to Poems (2020)
The Garden Black (2022)
A Specialist at The Recycled Heart (2022)
Ida: Searching for The Jazz Baby (2023)
From Volyn to Kherson (2023)
Alive Is What You Feel (2023)
White Whale (2024)
Pilgrim Volume 1 - Illustrated by Leanne Murphy (2024)
A Poetry Archive Volume 1 (2024)
A Poetry Archive Volume 2 (2024)
A Poetry Archive Volume 3 (2024)
A Poetry Archive Volume 4 (2024)

Picture Poetry/Spoken Image

Voices (In The Trash) (2020)
The Beechworth Bakery Bears (2021)
Sheep On The Somme (2021)
Waiting For Frank-Bear (2021)
A Lake Sambell Walk (2021)
A Few Places Near Home (2023)
The Cielonaut (2024)

What Readers Say

<u>*Small Town Kid*</u>

A modern-day minstrel. Highly recommended.
—A. F. (Australia)

Small Town Kid is a wonderful collection.
—S. T. (Australia)

<u>*Devil In The Wind*</u>

Trust me, this book will stay with you. Bravo!
—K. K. (USA)

Moving, beautiful, and terrible. I was left with a profound sense of respect, as well as a reminder that we should never take for granted every precious every moment of life.
—J. S. (South Africa)

<u>*The New Asylum*</u>

Words can't do justice to the emotional journey I travelled in (reading this collection).
—C. D. (Australia)

If I had to pick one book over the past year that has truly resonated with me, this would be it.
—K. B. (USA)

<u>*Walk Away Silver Heart*</u>

Instantly grips you by the throat in his step-by-step story of survival. Bravo!
—K. K. (USA)

Outstanding!
—B. T. (Australia)

A Kiss For The Worthy

A Celebration of Life Written in Thoughtful Bursts of Poetic Expression
—C M C (United States)

With every verse, I found myself reflecting about myself, my life, and the world.
—K

Rescue and Redemption

The passion of love in its many forms explored by one for another.
—J L (United States)

I've enjoyed every word, every breath. Every moment within the life of these stories.
—C D (Australia)

Sheep On The Somme

Museums and archivists take note--sell this in your gift shops, preserve it in your archives. Professors, teachers--share with your students.
—A R C (United States)

(This) book is a beautiful and graphic tribute to all those brave men and women who gave their lives for their countries between 1914 and 1918.
—R C (South Africa)

Ida: Searching for The Jazz Baby

I found myself deeply moved by the presentation of Ida's elusive, illusionary life.
—E G (United States)

He gives her a depth and vulnerability that the press didn't.
— A C (United Kingdom

The Garden Black

Prem creates verse that illuminates our world, its experiences and history.
—S C (United Kingdom)

Prem's poetry reminds that life is fragile and fleeting ... both harsh and beautiful.
—D G K (Canada)

A Few Places Near Home

The author has captured many beautiful images in this book, and is a wonderful photographer as well as a poet. This book would make a beautiful coffee table book filled with moving prose to make us ponder with gorgeous accompanying images.
—D K (Canada)

www.FrankPrem.com